QUIET MEN and THEIR COYOTES

QUIET MEN and THEIR COYOTES

poems

Mark MacAllister

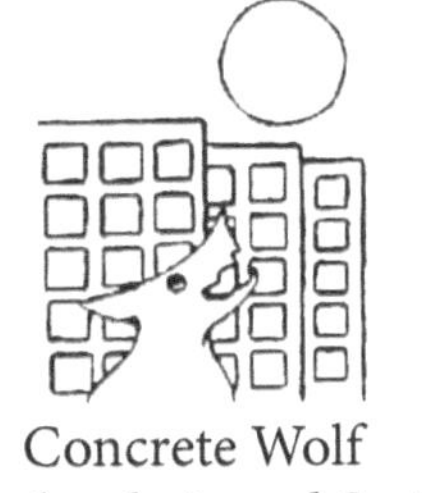

Concrete Wolf
Chapbook Award Series

Concrete Wolf Chapbook Award Series
Poetry
ISBN 978-1-936657-90-2

Cover art by Brian B. Beard

Author photo by Manon MacAllister

Design: Tonya Namura using Pompiere and Minion Pro

Concrete Wolf
PO Box 445
Tillamook, OR 97141

http://ConcreteWolf.com

ConcreteWolfPress@gmail.com

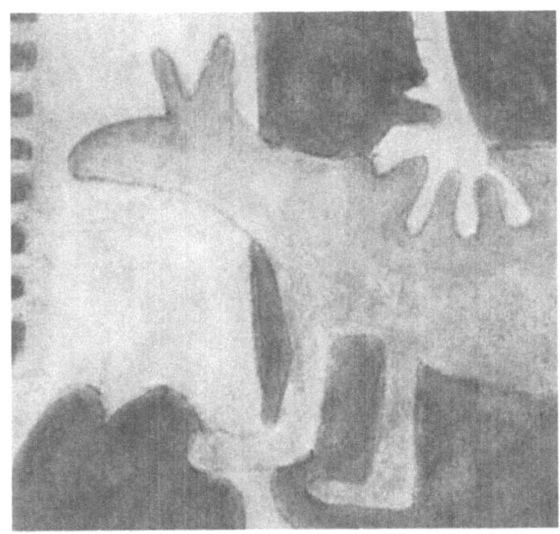

For my friends and colleagues at the Driftless Writing Center in Wisconsin and for those in the central North Carolina writing community. For Carolyn, Chris, Geoff, and Lisa in gratitude for decades of their friendship.

And, most of all, for Catherine, Manon and Cade.

Acknowledgements

"422 Trees" first appeared as "61 Trees" in *County Lines: A Literary Journal*, Franklin County (NC) Arts Council, 2021.

"Abandon" first appeared in *Deep Wild: Writing From the Backcountry*, Summer 2021.

"About the Poet" first appeared in *Passager Journal*, September 2021.

"Coyote on Wisconsin Highway 63" first appeared in *County Lines: A Literary Journal*, Franklin County (NC) Arts Council, 2021.

"The Days" first appeared in *Quiet Diamonds*, Orchard Street Press, 2022.

"Deer Crossing" first appeared in *County Lines: A Literary Journal*, Franklin County (NC) Arts Council, 2022.

"Lake Sixteen" first appeared in *The Journal of Undiscovered Poets*, 7MoreDays Publishing, 2021.

"Light Sleeper" first appeared in *The Journal of Undiscovered Poets*, 7MoreDays Publishing, 2022.

"One's Face at Birth" first appeared in *Steam Ticket*, Spring 2021.

"Rainbow Wilderness" first appeared in *Steam Ticket*, Spring 2021.

"The Road Is the Mules" first appeared in *The Journal of Undiscovered Poets*, 7MoreDays Publishing, 2022.

"Running Over With Coins and Bills" first appeared in *Steam Ticket*, Spring 2022.

"Shuttle" first appeared in *The Sixty-Four: Best Poets of 2018*, The Black Mountain Press, 2019.

"So Fast So Bright" first appeared in *Steam Ticket*, Spring 2022.

Contents

QUIET MEN and THEIR COYOTES

Where We Went When We Went Places

What comes to mind is our escape
from heat-waved Salt Lake City
through eastern Idaho
by nightfall Montana then three nights
of freezing rain in Glacier

while sleeping bags dripped in the backseat
we flipped an imaginary coin
decided to rush north and outrun the storm

turned right onto the main drag
in Babb a tiny border town
confused by the heavy traffic
the marching band in the rearview
we realized it was Babb's July 4th parade
and that the block-long line of classic cars
'57 Chevys and restored Mustangs
now included our Nissan Sentra

on to Alberta over a frost-heaved two-lane
the guard in the bright red customs shack
did not look away from his porcelain cup

next a deserted provincial road
we passed mile after mile of low dusky bushes
once pulled over we discovered ourselves
surrounded by wild prairie rose *Rosa arkansana*
none of it intentional or tended

we took it all in with just-married eyes
crushed the petals into our clothes
the skin behind our ears
guessed that those were Calgary's lights in the sky ahead

Shuttle

Friendships were like the days then
very short and tending toward cold
and I moved between both with a mindless plod
known best to the friend I saw yearly
as we passed on a Wisconsin path

late every November we started from opposite trailheads
met in the forest to swap keys
and then marched to the other's truck
fifteen minutes together over the nine-hour hike

the final one in a storm
the radio said stretched far into Canada
two thousand square miles beneath a single charcoal cloud
we agreed it a miracle
that the same snow icing the deck
of an ore freighter on Superior
melted on the eyelashes of a pretty girl in Thunder Bay

this day I'm alone among the familiar bogs and hemlock
dark before five and the coyotes hunkered down
the friend long gone to Thunder Bay
my dad's ghost hurries across a footbridge
under-dressed for the cold and anxious as always
he carries nothing to exchange
my route is toward where he comes from
and what is it behind me in the forest
that worries him so?

Light Sleeper

Require that your words behave when placed
            beside each other

feel free to drop *Ford Blue* next to *pickup* for example
but hold *rusty* or *ancient* for another poem

get straight your beliefs about snow

use *owl* and *mouse* but do not offer any details
about owls or about mice

decide where you stand when it comes to the body

be ready when the right word smiles down upon you

then and only then tell me about your truck
that ragged hole worn through the floormat
at the very spot where your clutch-side bootheel rests

about the doe and the wind-faced drift
that builds around her while she sleeps

tell me that a woman you know
wears between her breasts a long bright scar
            instead of jewelry

tell me how your Dad taught you to solder
to gap spark plugs and double-clutch a stick

tell me that you are a light sleeper
that you know the sound of an owl
when it takes a mouse in the woods
            just outside your window

how though it is muffled by the snow
it is enough to wake you

Lake Sixteen

A more thoughtful man would collect
          a precise few drops
in an appropriate vial and label each
for display where they could stay forever
cold and gin-clear

but what I prefer is to swallow
a few unfiltered and unwise mouthfuls
ignore the skating bugs   the tannin
beaver fever and the taste of tin

each wets the part of my brain
that recites lakes like a jesus prayer

Kawaguessaga is lovely second language
Namekagon and Shisheboganna   the names of sincere gods

soon we all will worship only water
at Lake Sixteen   which deserves a title more lyrical
I remained for hours
to witness a water dance of loons

returning to my truck in the near dark
a single snowflake arrived
(it would be a winter to remember)
and it fell so fast my tongue barely caught it

So Fast So Bright

I expect it was the Leonids
November 1999 just days after
          your brother's birth
though not quite four already you suffered
the first child's twin fears
of somehow being both in the way
and lost in the shuffle

so we gathered my safety orange Arctic bag
a groundcloth and red-filter flashlight
the stuffed animal specially selected
and chose our spot in the high school outfield

while I set up camp you in your parka
          and light-up sneakers
proved to me how fast you could run the bases
then stayed awake only for a few of the earliest

they were more numerous toward dawn
I watched one after another
at forty miles per second
cross the crescent-mooned sky
while you slept pushed down deep
into the cocoon I'd made for you

even your imagined friend
the one with whom you shared both a birthday
          and eye color
(you each observed the universe
through the same blue-going-on-purple irises)
the one you said kept thousands
of dolphins and sea lions as pets
was named *Star*

to this day I envy everything airborne
copy each year's showers
Lyrids   Taurids   Ursids
into my calendar
if for no other reason
than to remember they are there
undetectable in the middle of the day
but so fast so bright as we sleep

About the Poet

Thanks for asking
like you sixty percent of my body is water
raw milk makes up the rest
tinged blue and still steaming
          when brought in from the barn

I believe there are three types of rain
one barely breaks through the canopy
still it sounds like a river on the rise
another simply fails to arrive
          even though the lightning
the third is metal roof

finally you should know about the night I turned left
          from one gravel road onto another
how the headlights swept an unfenced pasture
two ghost white mules side-by-side and each hobbled
not a house or outbuilding in sight
the girl with rain slicker and boots though the sky was clear
her flashlight and the smell of pine trees recently cut
how it seemed that I would someday want to recall this
but only when someone asked me to

Keeping Warm in November

First-frost morning shoes wet
with the walk to the shed
lift the little space heater
from beneath the workbench
wonder as you have for three decades
if it will work through another season

rusted tan outer box ticks and twangs
the S-curved element inside goes red
and the weak fan comes on
five minutes later you shed your flannel shirt
crack open a window
breathe the burning-dust smell
leafpile kindling campfire
the woodburning tool you used years ago

•

In these days of freezing rain
take a garbage can lid
any pizza pans you can find
your son's round plastic sled
scatter them across the icy grass
fill them with sunflower and flax
stoke up the woodstove
from the window name the grateful birds

•

When traveling in November your first task upon arrival
should be to locate a switch for the small light over the
stove. Whether borrowed fishing cabin or executive suite or
one-night efficiency motel do not unpack until you know
where it is and if it works. When you go out leave the stove

light switched on as if someone had thought of you and
remembered before going to bed that you would be home
late that night.

•

There exists a few minutes
between near-sundown
and the stars' assembly
call it *gloaming* call it *twilight*
drive the dirt road into the woods
to where it dead ends at a wall of maple
take your seat on the tailgate
light the campstove make hot chocolate
call it *the end of another fine day*
your hands around the metal cup

"The flesh cries out for itself..."

I believe that line is Rilke's
though today I can find no evidence

someone told me the phrase
is in the bible actually
which means it is untrue

despite such uncertainty
who has not woken
to reach for another's hip

since Rilke was more than aware
          of the flesh
and obviously no fan of god
I'll trust it comes from him

though instead I could recall learning
to flush a deep wound with saline
to urge its edges gently together
until they meet like children
say twins reunited after
          a years-old tragedy

then run the needle through the skin
pull the line taut and again

with time the two
will knit themselves secure
healed in the manner we all heal
a single cell at first and again

the scar that finally binds them
is smooth and it shines
a language of their own creation
spoken by no other

422 Trees

I'm told there are 422 trees for each person on earth
this one has been split and stacked for me
by the tenth grader down the road

as it is rare to have a choice in anything
I examine each piece in the pile
choose two for the base
and a third to draw the fire up

the thin splintery twigs go in first
a slice of resin sticky as candy between them
smell of sap and flannel
then a flat smooth one to be propped up by the skinnies
an origin flame waves from yellow to blue
and soon the fire feeds on itself

how much longer can I pull this off
go out for another armload
     always a last one before bedtime
     always coatless for the chance to warm myself again
and then drop to the slate apron once more
on my achy atheist knees?

Ghost Ranch

—Box Canyon Trail/Abiquiu, New Mexico
(December 2021)

When you entered the canyon
between its open arms
it seemed much like a body

that the canyon exhaled for instance
its breath cold as cliffshade and snowmelt
though the day was a warm one

or that it was informed
as is your own body
by black bear and coyote scat
glitterstones and fragile purple flowers

and finally that you crossed and re-crossed
so many times the same narrow creek
that its route and yours came together helical
and what is that if not a body?

you drank at the canyon's terminus
a rockfall from centuries ago
as you shouldered again into your pack
another body came forward
ghost-slid its hands up between your arms and ribs
pressed a cheek to your shoulder blades

you held both wrists in an X
bent forward so its weight left the ground
only then did you remember the sharps of her hips

she breathed your ear *Careful don't drop me*
and through these many many years you have not

Abandon

The long-unused trailhead was exactly where promised
just past Hannah's Creek and marked by a tumbled cairn
the tread crossed by spider webs
and corkscrewed trees dropped by last year's storms

after three ridges it flattened out
the creek doubled back on itself to form a small island
and because I remember camps the way others
            do faces or birthdays
I knew this as a site I'd found more than half my life ago
mapless and with a woman I would discover
possessed the planet's loveliest hipbones

I have since learned two senses of *abandon*
one notes the joy of being profoundly unburdened
how everything we required then simply came to us
as if on the backs of the animals
that rested while we bathed in the waist-deep water

the other is to allow a place to go unvisited
to eventually forget it was ever there

Running Over With Coins and Bills

How is it this farm wagon came to be

How is it this farm wagon came to be marooned
alongside a less-than-traveled county road
thick ditchgrass waist-high
dry-honed sharp and moving toward seed

How is it this farm wagon came to be broken
once-red underskeleton and tongue sluffing rust
bald tires long-gone flat
spiral springs stuffed with rodent nests
deckboards the length of the wagon
parched-out gray and splintered

How is it this farm wagon came to be laden
with bushel baskets of carrots beets and onions
          peas and radishes and turnips
cardboard cartons of bush beans and tomatoes
antique glass bowls brimmed by cherries
apples and pears and six sorts of brambleberries

How is it this farm wagon came to be engraced
by the dented pie plate running over
          with coins and bills
a laminated handwritten sign

Honor Sistem!
Take what You need!
Pay what You can!
We are blessed and We are glad to share!

What Became Clear Today

—Birkhead Wilderness Area, 20 February 2021

Though I can no more resist a creek
than a creek can resist a river
my crossings have become clumsy
the water is higher
step-stones farther apart
and slicker than ever

When I am rushed my cursive
is often mistaken for my father's

Most men would gladly trade their scars for mine

A grad student collects deer ticks
there are frogs in the February mountains
something is wrong there is no doubt

The two tenets of my invented religion
don't crawl under fallen trees
because it is dangerous
don't climb over them   that is impolite

Know what the weather plans

Make clear to the forest your intentions

Eat well but save something for the squirrels

Cross at a bridge if you can

Finally a line is right only when it rings twice
once in the ear and then again in the mouth

The Days

—after hearing Ludovico Einaudi's I Giorni

Kind quiet people accompany you
the sort you would expect given their work
walk you to the overlook you requested
at creek crossings one takes your elbow

you are in a sweetspot
old enough that your children
no longer require you
but not so debased
that you would forego music or books

you settle onto a quilt in the leaflitter
consume what they prepare for you
they take your bruised hands in theirs

once they leave down the trail
you start the recording you brought
a modern piece   piano and strings
more sentimental than usual

here is the moment
you have been most curious about
what your thoughts will turn toward
now that it is irreversible

the smell of cedar and balsam to begin

how lovely it is the way mute animals
greet in this overwhelming forest

and then your first-born   your second-
how the backs of their heads warmed your palm

each time you brought their faces near yours
that those are the only days you'd beg to repeat

with that   finally   you are well

One's Face at Birth

As she flowed into the midwife's hands
Manon wore the expression of the front paddler
in a canoe about to pitch over a waterfall
as if her entrance into the world
was an ill-considered adventure
that still she did not intend to miss

whereas Cade arrived indignant at the injustice
of being pulled rudely through a narrow incision
into a brightly lit and very cold room
he looked like an angry bald man
arrested for a crime he did not commit

neither child has changed
my son's sense of fairness remains planet-sized
while his sister is the electric weather
that surrounds that planet

like most men of the era my father was not present
and my mother in no position to notice my first face
I suspect it showed both weary resignation
and the anticipation of things hypnotic
which makes sense as I was born
just three days before the fifties became the sixties

so here I am this many years later
it is early in an interminable January
ash-gray dusk and rainy
hands in my pockets and the trudge up the driveway
I stop short and listen
the year's first barred owl

Not Pointless or Too Greedy

The sun out and the wind up enough
to make the oaks shimmer
one barely dares to hope for days like this
a cold one so rare in April

you are on a roll now so go ahead
desire some other things while you can

begin with what you know is impossible
for example stop the bulldozers across the road
25 years ago there were just three houses
yours the Thomas's the Carter's
six adults and five kids all told
among 1100 acres of forest
now they are clearing a block of lots
as they did already to your north and your east
the 1100 has dwindled to
—what—
less than 100?

then hope for something that happened once
          but will not again
ask your Dad for help with the truck
he'll take a beer from the garage fridge
join you under the hood

There's a trick to it he likes to say
turn this screw a hair
hit that with a hammer
again and a little harder this time
OK try it

you reach through the driver window
twist the key until the big Ford turns over
he pulls the throttle back full and holds it there
until the tools vibrate on the walls

next hope for some thing that you find
            before you knew to look for it
limit yourself to a humble object
an arrowhead half-buried in the woodlot
a length of barbwire absorbed into a tree
no big deal but it reminds you
that others chose to remain in this place too

now for the end of the exercise

note the red-shouldered hawks moving
            onto your land
the ones from across the way
the ones chased off by the bulldozers

let them be what you desire

this is not at all pointless
this is not too late or too greedy

the trick is to decide that all you want
are the red-brown feathers
the banded tails
the high circles in the April sky

Quiet Men and Their Coyotes

Being curious coyote will follow
at a distance and for some miles
stop to drink at the creek long after you cross
trot to catch sight again

you both startle at the same wood grouse
bend to consider bear scat aside the trail
as expected he often wanders ahead
but the grass is matted where he waited

tonight as your one-log fire dims
reach deep into your belly and pull forth
a whine that drops hard into a howl
string it out long as you are able
until the hair on your neck lies back down
despite all the time spent together
this is the only sound you have offered him

coyote cannot resist and chuckle-barks an answer
then remembers to cut his voice short
you are surprised that he gave away his place
his heart breaks to learn you are as lonely as he is

Rainbow Wilderness

The Rainbow Wilderness loop is a commitment
ten miles in and only after you have noted piles of wolf scat
flushed grouse and crossed nine creeks
will you find yourself just short of halfway
as far from your truck as you will want to be
you now are in it for the long haul

a black bear browses in the frost-covered ferns
he moves like an old man
and clears a table set for autumn's visit
the guest that arrived late yet still departed early

when you walk into the bear's kitchen
he will gladly offer you a place
bring out the leftovers and then sit while you eat
he fixes his blurry eyes on you and asks

Do people believe you did enough for your Dad?

Whatever happened to that girl on the El train
the one who guessed it was your birthday
then kissed you just before her stop on Van Buren?

he watches you disappear down the trail
then gets back to his chores
with a headlamp and some luck you should find your
          way home
the long and coldest months are coming soon

Deer Crossing

Our road is lined with yellow metal signs
each reflects a lovely and leaping eight-pointer
a buck with a clear conscience

my daughter's first job was to help me
watch for deer when we drove at night
she leaned far forward in her booster seat
stared down the dark two-lane
just recently paved and yellow-striped

she could spot them atwitch in the shoulder weeds
or grazing in the neighbor's butterfly garden
the only one she missed ended up on my windshield

a county crew usually landfills the roadkill
though over the years I have shoveled several fawns
into the wheelbarrow when Manon wasn't looking

those that can crawl into the woods on their own
to avoid the bleed and burst on the hot asphalt
the vultures as they arrive are unnerved
when their wings tangle in the dense canopy
so they wait hunch-shouldered at the forest edge

then wrap their feathers like the darkest robes
proceed in funereal hops to the carcass
and all night take it apart as the cars hammer past
the children inside alert and lit softly as ghosts

Coyote on Wisconsin Highway 63

Song-dog   tall-eared eater-of-everything
I slow the truck and give a wide berth
so you can be safe in the other lane
from where you gaze at an empty house

you have just now understood
—indeed you somehow know this as luminous fact—
that the woman who would have loved you
lived there years ago

so many times you crossed this highway
crossed the pastures and dark forest edges
        now reclaiming the house
you decided it best to stay hidden

but she would have said your many names in a low voice
smoothed your nervous eyebrows
stepped naked across the room to find another
        quilt for the bed
while you learned to appreciate her drawings
to lie still and let her move an open hand
lightly across your throat

you shudder and twist hard as if to throw off water
        or to change the subject
what you've missed gathers around you like a small fog
then your muddy muzzle tilts up
and you go along sideways and southbound

Chamber Music

The bear has clumsy paws and he struggles to open the program. He is delighted to learn that tonight's concert will include Beethoven's Tenth String Quartet—the "Harp"—that he loves so. Sitting in the crowd of well-dressed and mostly older people, he is conscious of his musky odor, of the leaf litter caught in his coat. He is miraculously seated next to a lovely young woman. He is smitten with her and with the music they are hearing together. His eyes close halfway into the evening and his heart is happy.

For an encore the second violinist introduces a piece she wrote for her young daughter. It is harsh, atonal and abrupt. The woman next to him asks if he likes it. "No, not much," he says. "I have a daughter and that music did not make me think of her at all." Of course he has no contact with any of his offspring. But still he does wonder: *Would my daughter have any children of her own?* He imagines her quietly walking alongside a creek, her cub waddling beside her. *How did they manage this cold winter?*

The second encore is a sweet solo, a slow Irish ballad. After the audience applauds, the bear smiles and tells the woman "Now that reminds me of my daughter."

They get up to leave. He hopes she will invite him for coffee or even a glass of wine, as he would never even consider asking a young woman for such a thing. But that does not happen and he watches her long, black hair disappear into the crowd. He goes out a side door, cuts across the deserted grounds and into the woods.

He finds his bed of leaves and branches and tramps it down for the night, all the while reminding himself that longing begins in its own organ, one vital as the kidneys or lungs, and that it thrums on as thoughtlessly as they do, that it demands no more than steady blood and oxygen, and when it suddenly awakens it warms the entire body, and then he draws himself into a circle, covers his face with his paws, and dreams of his daughter, of dark-haired women, rivers and blood all flowing, the many souls that he loves and knows absolutely nothing of.

Hoof-Deep in Talbott's Creek

—Uwharrie National Forest, North Carolina
(August 2021)

The oldest mountains in North America
and today they look their age
wind-worn root and rock
creeks weak and petered out
now that it's late summer

mud at the Robbins Branch crossing
shows that others are also searching for water
skunk and squirrel tracks
then horseshoes oddly enough

there is water finally in Talbott's Creek
I spot him hoof-deep in the shade
tacked up and well cared-for
          at the mane and tail
he extends his neck to chew
the crazy grass on the shore

I hang a hammock downstream
wait to see who claims him
after four hours nobody has

he is leg-locked and snores
water weaves around his feet
I unbuckle the saddle
pull the bridle out of his teeth
flag-tape a note to the cantle
Been here since Saturday

it seems I should spend the night
(this may be his first outside a fence)
but stars and a cool dark breeze
bats that hunt in the canopy
will assemble to keep him company

though of course I wonder what he will do
should someone willing to deny him even that
arrive and lead him out of the creek

Problem Bears

The summer cabin people call me
about bears toppling garbage bins
cubs splashing in their hot tubs

my job is to use the dart gun
then tuck each animal in the too-small cage
for a ride deep into the safer mountains

while the bears forget quickly their ordeals
and return to the same spots
such events seem to stay with the tourists
How magical it is to see a bear they exclaim

for instance the young girl
who crawled into the rhododendron
to escape her quarreling parents

the small bear hiding in there too
made no move to frighten her
though he did say his usual grunts and huffs
when the adults found them together

this was so long ago but I expect
she is returned to that cabin by now
with no family as family is heartache
patient on the porch until the day
her bear pushes through the rhododendron

the sweet flowers shed the night's water
she welcomes him up and reads to him
while like it does every afternoon in the Blue Ridge
it rains for a calm hour

as his eyes close she looks out over the mountains
          and wonders again
what is wrong with her that she hoards her oneness so
wonders how it came to be that a bear
a black bear also alone and of a certain age
sleeps at her feet

Train of Thought With Whippoorwills

We commandeered a house
November my senior year
half-finished and abandoned
filled it with thrift store sofas
La-Z-Boys and loveseats

took care of it like our own
threw huge parties all winter
that I observed from a hammock
strung between two porch posts
beneath a quilt with a girl I had known
since we were in kindergarten together —

that house had rafters mitered the same way
as the ones in this Adirondack trail shelter
built by Boy Scouts it sleeps six
(though it is all mine tonight)
vault toilet out back and a metal bear box
short Milky Way walk to the creek —

from the floor I shine a flashlight up
to see what rodents scurry near the roofpeak
their eyes glow like the red-tailed monkeys
that lived in the grass roof
of my Ugandan forest hut
that jumped onto my cot at all hours
in search of apples and oranges
I'd hidden under the topsheet —

•

Are those whippoorwills
ever going to stop?

Frostbite

The steel can in the shed
meant to hold birdseed
had been empty for years
but when rolled on its edge
made the dragging sound of fingernails
across the bottom

beneath the lid nine possum joey skulls
each the size of my thumbprint
a scatter of other unidentifiable bones
small as those you would find in a baby's ear
too brittle and too delicate to bury
I dropped them into a glass jar
set beside a fawn's jaw

perhaps we hoard bones because they alert us
          to the idea of flesh
the way a cold day will wake one's frostbite
lead him to recall a drifted-over path out of the woods
upwind hand already gone hard and white
skin under the nails the same blue as the sky that day

seated near the woodstove I could finally flex my fingers
feel the cells inside begin to thaw
to thrum and surge like a nest of blind animals

Common Merganser

Shift down and slow
for the one-lane plank bridge
to your right a sight-line through the trees
just a portage path or deer trail really
offers a glimpse of the lake
something in the water
that you went by too fast to identify

if your daughter
say five years-old at the time
had been with you
she would before the end of the bridge
have concocted a heartbreaking story
a lonely duck abandoned
or separated when the flock
scattered at a gunshot

born six weeks early
four pounds and ten ICU days
she would decorate her horses
dozens of plastic appaloosas and palominos
with jewelry and stickers
insist they did not comprise a *herd*
but rather a *family*

and now at twenty-five
she still loves horses
wears a hard hat at the mill
watches over hot fierce machines
the size of a city block

knowing all that
stop the truck
it is a remote forest road after all
find the path and make sure

there he is with the green head
red bill and pillow-white body
even you can name him
common merganser

bobbing behind him
not a flock certainly but ducks enough
so that he is not alone
buffleheads and goldeneyes
mallards and more mergansers

hurry back to the truck
call your daughter at work
tell her what you first saw
what it then turned out to be

Is a Trick Of Light

> *The pigment in Blue Jay feathers is melanin,*
> *which is brown. The blue color is caused by*
> *scattering light through modified cells on the*
> *surface of the feather barbs.*
> —Cornell Ornithology Lab

Now you know for sure
that he is dusk-feathered actually
that his fierce cobalt duster
is a trick of light

as he knows now that what he assumed
to be a well-lit and unimpeded space
in fact is not

he thumped twice
loud but polite
first against the window
then onto the porch boards

  So sorry to trouble you friend
  he says in his brisk accent
  I don't feel quite myself
  might I just lie here a moment?

you two-hand him into a cardboard lid
on his right side as you found him
his left eye moves all morning

at noon you place him
on the passenger seat
explain that the forest down the road

(though many trees have burned
though the lake
which recently drowned in itself
has pulled back to leave
a ring of black stumps
gas cans and leaf rot)

is in fact quite lovely
when seen in the proper light

you park in the shade
set the lid on the tailgate
hike alone and think him gone
when you return to the truck he is

Sleeping Bear Pond

The woman headed toward me
asked about the trail to Sleeping Bear Pond
I pointed behind me then reminded her
of the shorter days these days
wished her good travels and continued on
we both were due somewhere before dark

she smelled of lavender and nothing but lavender
I am thankful to have been that close to home
as I lose all sense of direction
near a woman who bathes in lavender

I ought to have told her of the spot
near the shore and perfect for her tent
that faced the dark and humpbacked rock in the pond
how that rock is a rock and how it is also a bear

and let her know too that the bear sunned himself all day
that tonight's heat lightning
would reveal the many animals gathered to drink
how the sky would be blacker than any she's ever seen

that next morning the bear would wake
          and nose into the water
swim to the opposite shore then shake himself dry
stand and bob and weave
lift his muzzle to search for another bear
          to be a bear with
for the wildflowers that once filled this air
for all that he has learned to do without

The Road Is The Mules

Leave the certain trail
to follow instead the faint remains
of a mulewagon road
hacked through this forest two centuries ago
it switchbacks six-feet wide
along the steep hillface to the ridge
then down the backslope

the road is hand-cambered in places
to drain water and keep the loads level
pumpkins and sweet potatoes
splintered cedar bedframes and stacked deer hides
barrels of backwoods liquor
anything that could be sold in town

the road is the comings-and-goings
            of exhausted men
their wind-whipped women
against-the-odds children
all brief-lived and unrewarded

and of course the road is the mules
that slogged it into shape
near-starved and without fail worked to death
if they didn't die first by lightning or rockslide

at each cold creek crossing
the rare granting of a drink   a few seconds' rest
midstream water rising to their ribs
then the switch snap to the rump
the order to move forward
they came out shining on the other side

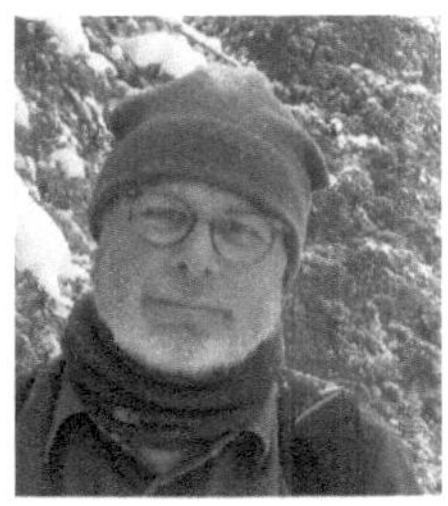

About the Author

Mark MacAllister grew up in northern Illinois, made frequent and formative trips to his grandparents' dairy farm in Wisconsin's Driftless region, and learned to write at Oberlin College. He lives in Pittsboro, North Carolina and continues to travel often in the Driftless area, as well as in Wisconsin's Northwoods and Michigan's Upper Peninsula.

His chapbook *The Field* was named a finalist in Variant Literature's 2020 contest, and he has twice been named winner of the "Carolina Prize" by the Franklin County (NC) Arts Council. Mark's poems appear in several journals, including *Steam Ticket, Quiet Diamonds, The Journal of Undiscovered Poets, Deep Wild: Writing From the Backcountry,* and *Passager Journal.*

For over 35 years, Mark's professional career has focused on the conservation of wildlands and wildlife. He is also an active member of his community's emergency response team, a board member of a red wolf conservation organization in northeastern North Carolina, and a board member of the Driftless Writing Center, a Wisconsin-based writers' cooperative.

www.ingramcontent.com/pod-product-compliance
Lightning Source LLC
Chambersburg PA
CBHW032131050726
47590CB00008B/3041

9 781936 657902